T0065572

FROM ROSES TO ASHES

From Roses To Ashes

A true story about Joy, Tragedy, Inspiration
and the Choices we make…

ANNA SHAW

PARTRIDGE

ISBN:	Hardcover	978-1-4828-8404-3
	Softcover	978-1-4828-8403-6
	eBook	978-1-4828-8402-9

COVER DESIGN AND BORDERS – Nirupama Francis
Silhouettes – Pramila Sekar

Print information available on the last page.

To order additional copies of this book, contact
Partridge India
000 800 10062 62
orders.india@partridgepublishing.com

www.partridgepublishing.com/india

Contents

Dedication

To my amazing children

Foreword

*L*ife is a mystery. It cannot be summed up in one sentence and anyone who is searching for the meaning of life will never find anything close to a satisfactory answer in their lifetime. The purpose of our existence is often tested by this entity called life. Sometimes it can be rewarding. At other times it can be unforgiving. It can take us to new heights of happiness or bring us to the depths of depression. It's behaviour is that of an emotional rollercoaster. How often have we come across the terms 'Life's good' or 'Life isn't fair'? Life plays the twin roles of a guardian and executioner. In the end, when we are in the position of taking our last breath, we reflect on the life we've lived and before we leave this world, we either are filled with satisfaction or contempt. But, I know for a fact that life is just a tool. It does not control us. It tries to. It gives us the impression that it is the puppet master and we have no free will. Nothing can be further from the truth.

I have seen the life of someone very close to me. You may have heard of her. She is the author of this book. I volunteered to write this foreword because I want to thank this person for showing me how to control life. She was able to do this with one very simple trick - living. I've seen her life. Her entire existence has all the components of a personal drama - family, wealth, intimacy, tragedy, failure, depression, elation, suicidal tendencies, hope, faith, religion, atheism and love. Watching her live her life has made me reflect on the choices I have to make for my future or more specifically, what not to do in life because the title of this book has a deep meaning. It is a metaphor for one person's descent from wealth and comfort to a life of insecurity and self-loathing and there is no one to blame, but the person who chose to make those choices. The lesson here is that even if you feel that life wronged you in multiple ways and played the odds against you, you can always fight back as long as you are alive or you can choose to succumb to the torture and live the rest of your days in contempt.

If you are someone who has lost hope, this book will put that back in you by showing you one regretful decision after another made by one person, so you realise that hope is that stubborn thing that will never die. If you are someone looking for direction, this book will show you the path not to take and if you are someone who is on the verge of losing hope, this book will set you straight and put you back on the path of happiness. Enjoy the book and take control of what is yours.

A friend

The quintessence of life belongs to the generous man, the giver. If the receiver is blessed, even more blessed is the giver. We never know how an act of kindness works. Often it goes full circle and impacts the very person who has been the subject of this act.

Sometimes what we get back is in direct proportion to what we have given. Never postpone kindness or compassion. Kindness symbolises a heart of generosity, compassion a heart of gold.

The Lonely Railway Station

$\mathcal{M}$y late father was the senior partner of a very famous catering business in Madras (now Chennai). He had a distinct position in this field and he changed the very scenario of catering in South India. Besides catering to visiting international and national dignitaries, his company was the official caterers to the South Indian Railways. Dad would often travel on the trains to oversee the arrangements and ensure that everything was perfect, since he believed that the hallmark of a good businessman was personal attention to detail.

On one of these catering stints something went wrong with the engine of the train. This problem could be rectified, but would take an hour or so, he was told. Night was falling when the train glided to a halt at a rather deserted station. Suddenly my father realised that he had been so busy that he had completely forgotten about his dinner. That particular day the dinner service had been overbooked and there was nothing to eat, and he was ravenous. He got down on to the platform wondering if he could grab a quick bite. Unfortunately nothing was available. Suddenly a young man came up to him and said something to this effect "Sir, how are you and what are you doing here?" Dad did not recognise the boy but did mention that he was desperately looking for something to eat. The boy told my father to remain where he was and that he would be back in about half an hour.

True to his word, he was back in hardly thirty minutes, carrying a "tiffin carrier" with the tantalising aroma of hot food, rendered more attractive, on this hungry night. It was authentic South Indian food, as delicious as it could get, but what my father enjoyed most was the steaming rice and pungent fish curry, obviously made with personal care. It felt like this was the best dinner my father had eaten in his entire life. After finishing the meal my dad was now comfortable enough to speak to the young man. The latter told him that a couple of months back he had stood outside a meals section restaurant in Madras, tired and very hungry. It so happened that my father was also the senior partner of this restaurant. When my father came out and saw the boy, he had enquired what he wanted. The young man told him that he was extremely hungry and that he had no money. Something sounded genuine in those words and tone, and so my father called one of his staff and told him to take the youngster inside and give him a complete meal. Eventually, his hunger had been fully satiated, and the grateful boy went on his way.

This was the same boy who served that hearty and delicious meal to my father at that lonely railway station on that unforgettable night.

The opulence of life does not exist in just palatial living spaces, but in living itself. The clinking of crystal, the rustle of silk, the fragrance of roses, the aroma of superb food, the laughter of friends, all point to a life of infinite opulence, to a distinctive lifestyle. These vivid and vibrant moments are etched in time and memory.

The Good Times

Dad was very fond of telling us the previous story and I never got bored of listening to it as he was a master at relating real life incidents.

Besides catering, he was also the senior partner of a ship chandelling company which regularly supplied the British ship S.S. Angela. Once in 21 days, she would sail from Singapore and dock in the Madras harbour and our company would take care of all supplies such as meats, pulses, rice, light engineering goods, wood and other non-specialised goods.

The S.S. Angela saw a long line of British Captains most of whom, if not all, became my father's close friends. My parents used to entertain them in style. You should have seen both of them, perfectly attired in their finery to entertain not only the captain but the officers as well, along with their own circle of friends! I can still smell the lavender water wafting from my dad and my mother would touch nothing but Yardley, a speciality in those days!

One of our dearest friends was Captain George Manson, and he used to actually stay with us for the three days the Angela was in Madras. I believe that I used to take him on a tour of our huge garden, including the backyard where my mother reared cattle for her milk business. When I met Captain Manson for the first time, my English was far from perfect. He challenged and inspired me to improve my English by the time he visited next. Winning the wager meant a visit for me to the Angela.

It was no surprise then, that in a short while my English improved greatly and my treat, was breakfast on board the Angela! Oh my goodness, what a sumptuous breakfast! The most exotic things were laid out on the table; there was a wide assortment of imported cheeses, meats, spreads, preserves, delicious beverages and a variety of breads. The highlight of the breakfast were the delicious fish cakes. Without exception, every get together on that lovely ship was remarkable whether it was breakfast, lunch or a dinner party. The ambience was very pleasing and everything was served with great warmth and hospitality

Captain Manson used to bring us the most fabulous chocolates from Singapore. Those days imported chocolates were an unheard of luxury. On top of this, he brought me books by Enid Blyton, my favourite author of all time. The world of fiction Enid Blyton created will always hold a truly special place in my heart.

I still remember Captain Douglas who gave me the most exquisite Easter egg I have ever seen in my life. It was a huge egg and the outer covering was made of delicious milk chocolate. Inside the egg, were neatly packed pieces of mouth-watering soft centre chocolates! It would not be an exaggeration to say that this was one of the best gifts I had ever received in my younger days.

We had a beautiful lawn in front of our home and the parties that were hosted there were the topic of much animated discussion among our neighbours, or so we were told. My father was a meticulous person with a fine touch and attention to the smallest details. He used to personally get the furniture arranged in small settings of one centre table with four chairs around it, of course with a vase in the centre, a vase of roses. The whole lawn was a visual delight and when the guests came in the night the whole place was glittering and pulsating with life. I wonder, do I still hear the clinking of crystal? My brother too had to do his part, but he used to get very upset, because every time my dad had a party, it would be on the day before his exams. With all these distractions I am amazed that he was a college topper.

My dad's parties were a great hit not just once, but every time, also because of the input from our catering department. We had extremely well trained waiters and superb chefs. But my mother's touch was evident for all to savour and enjoy! With her expertise in food and flavours, she served wonderfully versatile dishes, carefully selected to suit all palates. One of her popular specialties was crab meat baked in the shell, delicious enough to die for! For me it was a privilege to be part of those lovely days.

How beautifully life unfolds when you are young and transparent. Basking in the heat of a mid day sun, swimming in crystal clear waters, holidaying in cool hill stations, enjoying gastronomical delights; all this and more brighten up your day and cheer up your mood. These are the unforgettable thrills that fill the pages of your book of childhood memories.

More Good Times

The good times did not end with the Angela. My father had a weekend cottage at Ennore, a small fishing village some 20 kms from the city. He was a very keen angler. We too, would fish in the middle of the backwaters with his precious rods and reels, in our motor boat. We had some of the greatest times of our lives at Ennore with both family and friends. But the cleaning of the rods and reels after all the fun was over was a different ball game all together. It was tedious and time consuming. We had to be with him and help him rewind the fishing lines from the reels back to the spools and then clean all the rods and reels, till they were squeaky clean. I would vow never to go fishing again and yet the very next week end, there I was dressed in my khaki pants and shirt and huge hat raring to go! The best part of the whole exercise was that my mother would fry the fish we caught and serve it to us fresh and this taste was unmatched anywhere!

We also had a caretaker for the cottage, who, when sober, used to cook the most delicious food and a dish called Portuguese Fish which literally melted in the mouth. My mother learnt to make this superb Portuguese Fish. It is a filet of fish covered with, besides other ingredients, a mint and coriander chutney, packed in banana leaves and shallow fried. Recently I served this to my family but sadly, it was no match to my mother's cooking.

Our fishing expeditions were not confined to Ennore. One of the neighbouring states has a seaside town called Nellore. One Mr. Naidu owned a fishing resort on the other side of the backwaters called "Anglers Paradise" in a place called Krishnapattam. We would drive down to Nellore, leave our vehicles on one side of the backwaters and travel by boat to reach the resort.

Here, we had thatched accommodation which had a sense of exclusivity and down to earth elegance and comfort. We used to fish in the backwaters. I still remember my father warning me not to play in the water with my hand since the place was known to have sharks. The only thing that used to upset me was sometimes both my brother and I used to cast our fishing lines at practically the same spot just few feet apart. And he would catch all the fish and I would catch none. It was truly a paradise for anglers and I think one of the hardest moments for us was when we had to say goodbye to that great old gentleman and leave this never to be repeated experience.

Another place for us to unwind was the Madras Gymkhana Club. It would not be an exaggeration to say that I literally grew up here. I don't know why but my mother insisted that we ate only vegetarian food on Saturdays. My dad believed that Saturday was over at midnight. So on Saturday nights he would take us for a movie and then to the Gymkhana to have "Sunday breakfast". The club used to be kept open very late those days.

New Year's Eve at the Gymkhana was a gala affair with electrifying music and superb cuisine. I still remember one memorable occasion when we enjoyed ourselves so much that we got home only after 3 am, much to my father's chagrin. And during the summer vacations, when we were not holidaying, two of my friends, a cousin of mine and I used to get together in the swimming pool. We had loads of fun playing in the water and then sipping the oh-so-cool cricket drink that the Gymkhana was so famous for. I don't remember whether I was a good swimmer or not, but I have vivid memories of soaking in the spirit of those lazy summer evenings. As can be expected, such wonderful times cannot be without a downside, and I have to mention something that was not so exciting. We had great parties, wonderful weekends, and exciting holidays but it was not always easy on my mother. So things were not hunky-dory all the time. Both my parents were stubborn, short tempered people and when they got into a verbal fencing match all hell was let loose. But they couldn't live without each other. When my dad died my mother was inconsolable for a very long time.

School and college offer fabulous experiences not just in academics but also in exciting extracurricular activities. You should fully enjoy the innocent pleasures of childhood and in youth your life should be multifaceted. The taste of these days will linger for a long time even after life has moved on to other arenas.

School and College

*W*hen I was in the First Grade in school the teacher was very rude to me, so I complained to my father. Such was his influence in the city that the very next day I was taken out of the First Grade and put back in Kindergarten. But the following year I was back with the same teacher and I had to reluctantly deal with the pressure of it.

I joined an Anglo Indian School in the Fourth Grade. Besides my brother, a whole lot of my cousins studied here. So our family was well known in the school. The campus had two buildings, each spanning many square feet, situated diagonally opposite to each other, one for the girls and one for the boys. The whole lot of us cousins used to come to school in our bread van, as my father was also into the bread and confectionery business. When we passed the Boys school, they used to tease us shouting, "roti vandi!" "roti vandi!" (bread van) much to our amusement and sometimes embarrassment. Turbo charged as I was in school, I aced dramatics and other extracurricular activities. Ultimately I picked up the Head girl's trophy, a victory that thrilled my father.

When we were at school we had this family ritual of spending our holidays in the hill stations. Ooty or Ootacamund nestled in lush and verdant surroundings was my father's favourite spot. The Queen of the Nilgiris, as Ooty was called, was breathtakingly beautiful those days. What I remember about Ooty in my childhood was that every morning I used to climb into my dad's bed and lie next to him wondering what would happen if he suddenly died. I was so attached to my father that I could not envisage life without him.

My parents were part of high society and dad moved very closely with his lady friends. Once while returning from England, he came down the de-boarding ladder with one lady on each side. I was highly amused. His friends' wives would call him up both for business and social reasons and I was quite okay with that. You see, I had grown up in this kind of culture and I never gave it a second thought. As a daughter I was so broad minded, as a sister I was never possessive, but as a wife - I wonder what went wrong.

I believe my father was delighted when I was born. He considered me very lucky as he grew to greater heights in his business. I was a very plump baby with a head covered with curly hair and having no idea what was in store for me in the years to come.

Do you recall the unforgettable lines from Thomas Hood's famous poem "I remember, I remember" They go like this:

"I remember, I remember the house where I was born
the little window where the sun came peeping in at morn.
He never came a wink too soon
nor brought too long a day.
But now I often wish the night had borne my breath away".

That's what I wish too, that as a child before life corrupted me and shattered me with the greatest of all tragedies, the night had borne my breath away. But that was not to be.

Coming back to my childhood, I grew up in a huge house. My father pampered me to the hilt. When I was in school I actually had a governess for a short while and was the given a pony to ride, whose name was Humpty Dumpty. I remember an overweight cousin of mine who wanted to ride him. He got on to the pony from one side and went tumbling down the other side. It was so funny that I laughed till I could laugh no more. And in the evenings my favourite waiter Loganathan from our catering department used to walk with me around our garden calling me "Baby" all the time and took care of me with so much affection. Loganathan kept in touch with me till the very end of his life.

I have to mention that when I was a teenager my parents were very well known in the city's social circuit. There came so many proposals of marriage for me. I would just laugh them off, but one was interesting. I must have been hardly eighteen when we got this proposal from a well known family and the boy was supposed to be "Adonis" himself. I must confess I was curious to see him, but all my hope went up in smoke when we came to know that this "Adonis" was an alcoholic. Believe it or not, every time the phone rang, I used to think, oh God, not another proposal! To add more amusement to my life, some of my father's closest friends insisted that I was going to be their daughter in law. None of this, however, affected me and I finished school with a First class and the highest marks in English.

Those days we merely applied and got seats in college. I joined one of the most prestigious colleges in the city and had a wonderful four year tenure. For three years continuously I was Class Representative. I hate to admit this, but my grades went down. I hated Sociology and Economics but loved History. At college everything was on my agenda, except academics. The premium was on winning, whether it was oratorical contests, dramatics, short story writing, one had to win, and I won ever so many times. Life, however, was nothing short of a roller coaster ride because I was not smart enough to balance academics and extracurricular activities, which my friends did so beautifully. I thankfully just managed to get my Bachelor's Degree, and I told myself that I would never enter the portals of another college ever again. Yet a year later I was back at University to do my Masters in History. I joined a primarily boys college where women were admitted in the Post Graduate section only. The History department was well known for its fabulous faculty. I loved my two years stint and since there was hardly any competition, I was known as the "Natural Beauty" of the college! I won a short story competition and was thrilled when the story was published in the college magazine. Up to date, it is one of my favourite pieces of writing.

Again, I mention in detail my charmed and privileged childhood and youth, as I felt none of these came to my rescue at crucial times later in my life when life's choices loomed overwhelmingly in front of me. I even felt I allowed myself to not take pride in my appearance, and lost my sense of self worth, in spite of all my promising upbringing!

It is not the kind of work you do but how you do it that really matters. With the right attitude the most strenuous jobs can bring you great pride and satisfaction. To respect dignity of labour is the mark of a real person.

Dignity of Labour

$\mathcal{M}$y parents brushed aside all rules of the higher echelons of society when they decided to turn their hobby of fishing into a business. So every time there was a good "catch" we would get a phone call and even if it was midnight my dad would drive down to Ennore in his van and pick up the seafood. Incidentally the village headman was one of my father's closest friends. The fish business entailed a lot of hard work. My parents themselves would cut and slice the fish. They were experts at this. There was no dearth of demand for fresh catch. Needless to say, many of our friends would walk away from our home with free fish.

To be frank, I was then a little ashamed of them selling fish. But the realisation that this was nonsensical thinking came to me in my later years, when I came to understand the concept of dignity of labour and I valued their honest enterprise. It was a humbling experience to remember how my parents engaged in physically strenuous work, and to reminisce now with a sense of pride.

When I was doing the second year of my Masters, we saw some very bad times in business. We were doing so well in our catering and confectionery business as well as the ship chandelling. Then my father and his brother diversified into the plywood sector with the help of an Italian gentleman who brought Italian technology to our manufacturing unit. It began with flush doors and then went on to include other wooden structures. The factory was located in a huge piece of land. We also toyed with the idea of building a house adjacent to the factory and moving there. But the whole enterprise was a failure. This was the beginning of the downward trend in our lives, which we had never experienced before.

Then they diversified into the manufacture of ceramic tiles. This time our collaborators were Japanese. The way the Japanese worked to set up the factory was mind boggling. But problems set in once again and the factory had to be sold. The losses were enormous. Simultaneously my father became unwell. My brother took over my dad's problems and responsibilities which were staggering. He sent my parents to recoup in a relative's farm, some 100 kms from Chennai for six months. The six months dragged on to become eight years. My father however, did not sit idle at the farm. He tilled the land, driving the tractor himself and my mother cooked the food for the farm hands initially on firewood. The transformation of their ordinary residence into a lovely farm house was the result of my father's sense of innovation and good taste. I stayed back in Madras with my brother and sister in law. I was very attached to my brother's family. I visited my parents occasionally. Even in the farm, my mother fed us sumptuous meals, while I spent most of my time reading.

One day, my parents were at the petrol pump filling gas for their vehicle. They saw some old friends on the other side of the gas station. They started walking towards them, when the latter just got into their car and drove away. These were the very same people who had been wined and dined by my parents, not a long while ago. My parents were bound to have been shocked and hurt by this indifference. Today my parents are no more. I want to dedicate this chapter to their memory and the lessons that can be learnt from their lives. They did not allow society to set the parameters of their lives. They lived life on their terms, with a lot of support from my brother. No wonder then, that to this day, they are remembered with great affection, by those who matter - their family and true friends.

The unicorn is breathtakingly beautiful. But do not search for this lovely creature. It is impossible to find. It lives in the realm of imagination.

The Proposal

Strangely enough my mother never showered affection on me when I was young. Her blue eyed boy was my brother, about seven years older than me. And strangely enough that did not bother me. I adored my brother. Right through my childhood, youth and adulthood he has been my greatest pillar of support. My father adored me but I was unhappy with some of his business moves and this smothered my affection for him. He knew something was missing in our relationship, but he let things be.

While my parents were at the farm, some people close to them were worried that I was refusing to get married. They were not aware of the fact that I was waiting for someone specific. The story goes that one day at the farm, my parents received a telephone call from one of our close and dear relatives who was one among the most respected members of the family. She was very keen that I marry one of her grandsons. My father was very happy with this proposal, and so was my mother, since the boy was well known to my family. He was a very good looking and dashing young man, a man many women would kill for. I too was interested but wanted to meet him and have a talk before taking a decision. He was in the USA and expected to return to India in six months time. Six months later, they said he was coming back in just over a month's time.

My parents expressed concern over this delay, as they had rejected several other proposals. "Just a month's time," they said, but time went on and on. My brother correctly sized up the situation and wanted me to meet other eligible bachelors, one or two of who were actually keen on marrying me. I did feel the pressure, but I was stubborn and refused. I took the risk of waiting for him for five years and he remained as elusive as ever. With so much time gone by, suddenly every phone call was not a proposal any more.

Problems must be looked upon as challenges to test our mettle. Whether we believe it or not, we all have the strength to face trials and tribulations. We must draw upon our inner resources in difficult times. When we find relationships are no longer meaningful, we must muster the courage to walk away. Unsteady relationships lead to volatile marriages which cause chaos to children with young developing minds.

The Meeting

*H*aving finished my Masters, I taught high school youngsters for a while, and appeared not too successfully in the IAS (Indian Administrative Services) exams and finally landed a job of a copy writer at an advertising agency.

A couple of days later I happened to come to office later than usual, feeling unusually light and happy. I sat down at my desk and was about to start my day when a really handsome man walked out of the chief's office. He went to the telephone and made a call. Must be a client, I thought to myself. While I was still marvelling over his looks, he was at my table saying some oft used line, like "haven't we met before?" That was the beginning - the turning point in both our lives.

He was in the client servicing department. We got to know each other pretty well and fairly soon. Did we fall in love with each other? To this day I don't have an answer. But in the whole spectrum of my experience I had not moved so closely with any other man. I began to feel more energetic and accomplished and looked forward to each day. Maybe it was this early euphoria that led to marriage. He was a very friendly person and cordial to both men and women. His exceptional good looks, easy charm and friendly personality made him very appealing, especially to women. Maybe unconsciously I resented this attention to other women. I really don't know. This was in spite of the fact that he wanted to marry me but did not force me. It was a joint decision. Unfortunately I began to doubt whatever he told me. We should have ended our relationship then and there. But we did not. Did I make life's greatest mistake by not parting as friends once the poison of suspicion entered our lives? I foolishly believed that things would get better after marriage, but of course, they seldom do. And in my case they definitely got worse. The arguments started and I was very upset with him. So I decided to change my job.

I walked through an interview into one of the biggest ad agencies in the country. But I didn't make it as a copy writer, due to my own reservations. When I was asked to develop copy for the launch of a new restaurant, since my family owned a couple of restaurants in the city I believed that this was tantamount to disloyalty.

Once again, I reiterate that the day I changed my job, he and I should have parted as friends. So much sorrow could have been avoided. There were so many issues in our married life, that sometimes we were not even cordial to each other, let alone affectionate. His point of view was that I smothered all his feelings with my suspicion. Maybe he was right. I saw him in terms of what I wanted him to be, not what he actually was. Unfortunately, the thread of suspicion was present throughout the initial years of our life together. It was not just both of us but our two children who got entangled in its vicious grip.

Family relationships are the mainstay of society. The stability of these relationships sometimes depends upon certain moral rules which are religious in nature. Unfortunately certain people use these rules to treat others harshly. This is very disturbing especially to brides who are new comers to the family. It is demeaning to religious beliefs when they are used as instruments to lower the dignity of fellow human beings.

The Ramifications of Caste

*I*f some countries are still racially insensitive in this day and age, India certainly still suffers from the ramifications of caste. Caste prejudice however does not reflect the values of sensible Indians. The caste system in India was originally a segregation of Hindu society on the basis of livelihood. On the top rung of the caste ladder were the priests and scholars who were well versed in prayer, rituals and literature. Next came the political leaders and warriors. They were followed by the merchants. Finally came the labourers, peasants and servants. They were considered lower in stature by the other three classes. There was also a fifth and last segment though Hindu law books do not mention a fifth category. They were the people who did menial tasks such as scavenging and were thus termed "untouchables". These unfortunate people had no access to Hindu shrines and were subjected to unspeakable atrocities. What is shocking is that even today caste in all its horror is prevalent in rural India. Caste sometimes raises its ugly head even in urban society.

When I got married I had no inkling that I was going to suffer the trappings of the caste system. It came as a complete shock when I did. I was supposedly "lower" than my husband in the caste hierarchy. I had no idea and my husband did not educate me that his mother was an extremely orthodox lady.

He really believed that she would look after me like a daughter. Unfortunately that was not the case. In all honesty having had a very liberal upbringing I had no idea of the meaning of orthodoxy. So my mother in law's treatment towards me came as a rude shock. Even a meal was not served in a friendly atmosphere since my way of handling food was wrong in her eyes. In sheer frustration I missed many a meal.

There were other issues as well. Hindus perform rituals for those people who have passed on. On the eve of the ritual for my late father in law, my mother-in-law implied that my presence would contaminate the ceremony. So she suggested that I spend the night and the following day with my parents who had relocated to Chennai from the farm. But I did not want them to know anything of the problems I was encountering at my house. I did not leave the house that night but early next morning I took a bus trip around the city to kill time until it was time to be at my place of work.

During another ritual I was not allowed to enter the kitchen because the so called "high caste" cook took objection to my presence.

But there was a silver lining – my husband's grandmother. She was a wonderful lady and very fond of me, right from the start. She treated me with a lot of affection. But she did not reside in Chennai.

My father's heart broke when he eventually came to know what was happening. The stress caused me to develop anaemia, a condition which continued into my first pregnancy. I had to move in with my parents as the doctor felt that being anaemic was not good for the baby.

A few years later, suddenly, my mother in law changed completely. All orthodoxy was thrown to the winds. There was a reason for this total transformation. There was an inter-caste marriage within the immediate family which was conducted with my mother-in-law's blessings. She threw aside the mantle of caste when it suited her. But she had no second thoughts about disconnecting me from my dignity, and from my self-esteem as a human-being.

My husband feels really bad about his mother's attitude towards me in the earlier years. He tried to convince me that it was her insecurity that made her do what she did. I have no idea whether he was right. She did not realise that kindness would have conquered me totally. But today she is genuinely sorry for her past behaviour. Now she treats me with a lot of care and concern. I really appreciate that.

It is now an established fact that the art of appreciation can bolster our physical and mental well being. Appreciation is the missing link in many relationships, especially marriage. No one likes to be taken for granted. When a man says 'thank you' to his wife, in all probability she will willingly return the compliment. Such a simple act of gratitude goes a long way in cementing interpersonal relationships. The sad fact is that the little things in life are seldom given due importance.

The Eternal Need for Validation

People say the charm of marriage sometimes dies down after just a few years. In my case I wondered if there was any charm at all. One day we attended the wedding reception of one of his colleagues. Immediately he commented on the good looks of the bride. He had not even noticed how well dressed and good I looked. So what had happened to make him notice her and not me? He was thoughtless, even cruel, I would say. But I was a fool. I put away all the lovely clothes I had bought for my wedding and let them rot. They went to pieces. I let my insecurities handicap me.

This was not all.

He was impressed with the lady we met while house hunting, as she was a great housekeeper and maintained her home perfectly. I felt these comments were aimed at making me feel less competent.

Let me add one more incident. A famous movie star's wife was selling advertising space to corporates during the launch of her husband's much hyped movie. My husband worked for one of the corporate houses vying for ad space. And all that he could tell me was how wonderfully efficient Mrs. Famous actor was and what a marvellous business woman!

Does this seem silly and childish? Is there any wife who does not appreciate compliments from her husband? Is there any wife who can tolerate frequent adulation of other women? That being said, all that my husband could have done was to first compliment me on how good I looked or how well dressed I was or whatever! Believe me I have had my share of compliments from others. If he had done that I am sure I would not have minded him complimenting other women. But he did not. And so another issue came up in our already volatile and unsteady relationship.

I could have done another thing. I should have taken my husband's attitude as a challenge and ventured into a career. But I threw everything to the winds and became a stay at home wife, who lost all self esteem. What happened to all the confidence of my younger days? No doubt I had come a long way from a glorious past but I should have carried the spirit of my childhood with me. Had I shown a different side of my character perhaps I could have been empowered enough to hold my own and gain the respect that was duly mine.

Or was the universe balancing my life by showing me the other side of the coin?

In all fairness to my husband he did not grudge me a career. In fact years back I had written a short story which had a really unexpected ending. My husband sent this story to a competition organised by a famous Asian magazine. My entry was adjudged as one of the fifty best stories in Asia and I was offered the post of a sub editor. This job meant relocating to Hongkong. Both my father and my husband were excited about this offer and were very keen on my family going to

Hongkong. I weighed the pros and cons of the situation. I refused to shift from Chennai. I did not want to leave my little son's paediatrician.

Some people are unflinching in their devotion to their parents. Yet others do love their parents but there are constraints in demonstrating their feelings. Good parents understand and let things be, secure in the knowledge that their children nurture love for them in their hearts.

Of Fathers and Daughters

*A*fter my second delivery my father starting ailing. It slowly escalated with time. He started suffering from severe and constant stomach pain. But we as a family never realised the fatality of his pain. In fact the Histopathology report had shown benign results. One night my father cried with pain and I cried too. I comforted him saying that though his pain was a terrible thing, it would pass. His pain never passed. Acute pain should be investigated and at least the cause of the pain must be identified. Pain should not be allowed to spiral out of control.

My father was admitted into a hospital with acute pain. By the time he was put on the operating table it was too late. When I walked into the ICU (Intensive care unit), I got a dreadful shock! I could not believe my eyes. My father was sinking. Then and only then did I realize how critical he was. Then and only then did I realise, after many years, what my father meant to me. I rediscovered my love for him in that ICU. So much had to be spoken. But my father was in no condition to listen, much less talk to me. The unsaid words remain unsaid forever. On the fifth day we got the absolutely shocking news that he had advanced stomach cancer. The downhill trend started immediately and his condition deteriorated rapidly. Even then I did not give up hope. I went from one place of worship to another place of worship. But it was all futile. Even the all forgiving Lord who actually died on the cross for the sins of us mortals did not show mercy on me and spare my father. My father slipped in to a coma and I was hanging on to the last straw within my reach. I was trying to seek the intervention of a "God man". I returned home around 7 pm. There was something strange in the atmosphere in the room. My husband asked me to come upstairs as he wanted to show me something. Half way up the stairs I suddenly stopped. "Is it pappa" I asked.

My father had passed away on that day. No doubt it was a terrible loss for me. But it was my children who were affected the most. They lost a grandfather who had adored them, who would have done anything for them, who would have impacted their lives. But unfortunately, that was not the way life played out for our family. However I must express my deepest gratitude to my late mother. She was a remarkable lady with indomitable will power. Her very presence gave a lot of courage to my family. Her personality infused strength into the lives of my children. But she would often reiterate the fact that my father's presence would have had a far reaching impact on their growing up years. Despite the fact that she was reeling under her own sorrow she did not give up on life. I celebrate her unforgettable role in our lives.

Contrary to what we think the world does not contain all the answers. Sometimes we have to pick the right option ourselves, sometimes collectively. To come to a decision is to take on responsibility. People are often frightened to shoulder this responsibility. They seek a solution from others. Refrain from putting the onus of accountability on someone else. Weigh the pros and the cons of the situation and make the choice with serenity and strength. You can do little else.

Don't Push the Panic Button

Some parents become totally irrational when their children fall ill. They become so emotionally stressed out that the poor kid is more frightened of his parents than of the illness itself. They confuse themselves and sometimes unfortunately the doctor himself. When my elder son was quite young he developed high fever with an excruciating headache. I tried to diagnose the ailment by asking the doctor whether it could be meningitis (brain fever). My doctor was thinking on different lines but this question put an iota of doubt in his strong mind. He started treatment as per his diagnosis which he did not reveal to us at that point but decided to perform the L.P. (Lumbar Puncture) the following morning. At that time, this was a terribly painful procedure where fluid is collected from the spine. The result was immediate. It was not brain fever. By the evening other results came in confirming my doctor's diagnosis of acute sinusitis, for which medication had already been started.

My poor son had been unnecessarily subjected to unbearable pain. The doctor told me in no uncertain terms that he did not want me to do any diagnostic work for him in the future.

Now let me take you to a completely different scenario.

My little niece had developed Jaundice and we gave her sips of cold water to alleviate the nausea. Unfortunately this affected her throat very badly. It was so severe that she had to be examined by an ENT specialist. He told the already distressed parents that it was probably diphtheria, a terrible disease and she needed an injection straight away. She was also to be tested for the disease but the injection could not wait till the results came in next morning.

We decided to take a second opinion and took her to her own paediatrician. He was confident that it could not be diphtheria as she had been given her immunisation shots as per schedule. Further, those days the diphtheria injection was a large and painful one which given once could not be repeated.

The parents were in a real dilemma, did they shout and scream? No. The three of us, my brother, sister in law and I carefully discussed the issue in a calm manner. We put our faith on our paediatrician and decided not to give the injection till we got the lab results. The next morning I drove down to the laboratory and collected the report. It was not diphtheria.

Please note this important point. The reason for recalling this incident is not just a medical one but also an emotional one. There is no doubt that both the situations were very disturbing. But what is the point of getting emotional and frightening the patients, especially children, who need comfort and kind words and not drama. At the same time I have no intention of saying that the paediatrician was more skilled than the ENT specialist. In fact, our paediatrician was highly acclaimed in his profession and so was the ENT specialist in his. It could have gone either way. It was lucky that the decision taken turned out to be the right one. This in no way reflects on the ability of the ENT specialist. What is important is such decisions should be taken with a calm and stable state of mind. The decision should be taken after much thought, collectively if need be, and the rest left to God.

There are people who do not advocate sparing the rod and spoiling the child. They argue that sometimes the best of youngsters emerge from homes where the rod is used. Be that as it may, but do two wrongs make a right? No child should be beaten. At any cost an act of violence unleashed on an innocent child is a crime that deserves no pardon.

An Unforgivable Act of Violence

Siblings have funny relationships. They love each other, some adore each other, and some tolerate each other. And there are others who hate each other or think they do.

My elder son, when a child, had this funny way of expressing his affection for his younger brother. He would give him a tap on and off. One day he tapped him too hard and the latter started yelling. This upset my husband so much that he nearly lost his temper completely. But he controlled himself and told our elder son not to unnecessarily trouble his brother. He showed great restraint in not hitting his son for whom he had really very deep love. The feeling was mutual.

I must tell you what I did to my elder son one terrible night. I was in a foul mood and very upset over something. I went in to one of the rooms where my son was lying down on the wooden floor with a torch he had so artistically and totally dismantled. He lay there with a guilty smile on his little face. Did I smile back and share this precious moment with my child? No, I did not. I lost my reasoning completely and gave him two kicks on his back - an incident that has never left my memory.

I immediately got very frightened about whether I had injured him. I rushed to my husband and told him what I had done and that I wanted to see the doctor immediately. My husband was furious with me and refused to come to the doctor. So I bundled my son up into an auto rickshaw late at night, and rushed to the paediatrician's house. He was woken up. He examined my son and fortunately nothing seemed wrong. But he was very shocked, as he did not expect such behaviour from me. At this juncture, I think my husband joined us.

The next day, when I told my brother what had happened, surprisingly he did not find fault with me. He told me that sometimes parents do terrible things but it does not mean that they do not love their children. I was someone who believed that hitting children exhibited unbridled violence. In fact at my children's school, I had many times spoken about the disadvantages of corporal punishment. I used to get terribly upset if I came to know that my children had been beaten at school.

How could such a person commit such a horrendous act of violence? The fact that I had kicked the person I loved most in the world will always haunt me.

To this day, in my mind, I stand in the court room to hear the verdict - Guilty! GUILTY as charged!

Words have both the explosive power of a thunderstorm and the soothing effect of balm on a bruised wound. They can bring tears to the eyes or a smile to the face. They are like swords which are weapons of honour or of destruction. Choose your words with caution, especially when directed towards children.

The Chocolate Sundae

We were a group of family and friends having had a get together at a popular restaurant. The whole dining experience was to be a memorable one. We all felt that the evening would be incomplete without us ordering desserts. We all ordered our fantastic desserts – ice creams, milk shakes, double and triple sundaes and what have you! Suddenly I saw my elder son enjoying a chocolate sundae. He was leaving on a school trip in about three or four days. Seeing that he was having a "cold" dessert suddenly shook me up. I immediately went up to him and scolded him for being so reckless. He pushed his sundae away and sat silently while the rest of us including me finished our delicious concoctions.

You should have seen his face! It was a picture of mortification. I don't think that not being able to finish his dessert distressed him as much as the fact that he had been humiliated in front of family and friends. The least I could have done was to tell him quietly not to have a cold dessert as he might fall ill before his school trip. And to share his disappointment, I too should have given up my dessert. But, alas, I did just the opposite. I wonder how long my son nursed his grievance. He never mentioned the incident to me. I regretted my behaviour but spoken words cannot be taken back, nor can humiliation.

Gurbaksh Chahal, tech entrepreneur who has built three ad networks dropped out of school at the age of sixteen. His current companies' net worth is half a billion dollars.

Evan Williams, Biz Stone and Jack Dorsey all dropped out of different universities and created --------TWITTER!

Am I advocating that children drop out of school and college? Definitely not. But why this torture over grades?

The Torture of Grades

Examinations can become very stressful for both children and parents if not handled properly. Unfortunately parents have given grades a false importance of impacting their children's careers as well as their lives. Obviously they're not aware of some of today's top notch entrepreneurs who have dropped out of college and even school. Some years back my elder son had just received his board exam results. He had cleared the tenth grade with an average of 79%. His friends had all fared better with 80's and 90's. I was so upset that I scolded him and told him that if he had put in more effort he would have done better.

I rang up one of my close friends to tell her the bad news. She was absolutely shocked by my attitude and reprimanded me. She told me that I should look at 79% as being one percent less than the 80's range and should have actually congratulated my son. Further, she continued, even if he had scored lower marks, it did not matter, as low or high grades were not the end of the world. I called my son and shocked him by congratulating him saying that his marks were really only one short of 80! And that this actually called for a celebration. The poor boy could not believe what he was hearing. It seemed so irrational on my part to first reprimand him and later congratulate him. A matter of one percent had brought on this anger. And even if he had got lower marks, what did it matter? Even if his grades had been in the 40 -50 range, the most appropriate course of action would have been to sit down with the child and discuss future assistance or tutoring.

How many parents do this? The need to excel is driven into the child's head so deeply that in sheer frustration of not having fulfilled their parents' wishes some children actually contemplate suicide.

Are grades more important than a child's life! Parents must learn to accept both success and failure; failure with compassion and success with humility.

But what is so inspiring about this incident is that I completely changed my stand on grades and I no longer consider it a yardstick of intelligence. In fact, it was a complete transformation for me. I never reprimanded my children ever again on their performance in school or college. Over the years I gained their confidence to the extent that they could come to me with any problem, grades related or just about anything at all. I became their friend.

Everything you are today, your lifestyle, your status, your dignity is in some way or other rooted in money and property. Whether you like it or not whether you accept it or not money is essential for your existence, for your children's tomorrows. Spend wisely but don't compromise on comforts and affordable luxuries. Never act first and think later. Make sure that every financial decision taken by you is rooted in common sense with input from those who know the game.

Financial Disasters

$\mathcal{H}$aving gone in depth into the good and bad times of my life, I want to explore an area that affects most people, money and property. My father's property was developed by some well-known builders. I was given a spacious three bed room apartment which I chose to rent and live in a smaller flat. My late father in law had left behind an independent house in a lovely residential locality. At some point in time the family wanted to come to a settlement. My husband's mother wanted a certain amount of money in lieu of which she was willing to transfer the house to her son. The transaction required the consent of her two daughters. While the younger daughter was only too willing to oblige, the elder one created some problems. Any way the "No objection" papers were finally signed. Unfortunately my husband and I could not manage to obtain the necessary money for the settlement and his mother would not lower the amount due to various reasons.

Then another proposal to develop the property was put forward. We would get a spacious apartment and my mother in law would be given a smaller but equally good one. Unfortunately she wanted a bigger flat and some money on hand. This was just not possible. Thus a brilliant idea was thrown to the winds. Finally and tragically my father in law's hard earned legacy was sold. After giving the promised amount to my mother in law, we went on a feverish spree of house hunting to avoid a tax called capital gains. We identified a flat in a multi unit complex. But we ran short of the money required. Taking a home loan did not seem a good or feasible idea at that point in time.

I committed one of the biggest mistakes of my life by selling the flat given by my father. The shortfall in the purchase of the new apartment was thus managed by the sale of the flat sentimentally gifted by my father. I was left with some money which I invested and later spent it on education, travel and so on and so forth.

We rented the new apartment and continued to live with my mother. Some years later my husband got a new job with a very attractive HRA (House Rent Allowance). We moved into a beautiful ground floor apartment which was more like an independent house with all the benefits of a multi unit complex.

Things went smoothly for a couple of years. Until there came a time when our own flat was without a tenant. My husband wanted to move to his flat but strangely enough my sons and I had developed a dislike for the building. So I decided to sell the flat and buy another one which would suit us. Once again I committed a terrible mistake by selling the flat without identifying alternate accommodation. We just could not find the right flat though we checked out more than thirty properties. Time flew by, real estate prices sky rocketed and we were left with a small amount of money which was nowhere near the value of our former apartment. The outcome of all these impulsive decisions was that in the place of three individual properties we were left with just one apartment which was incidentally gifted by my brother. The onus of accountability undoubtedly lies with me.

We have two mental faculties, the mind and the intellect. Our actions can be driven by the whims and fancies of the mind or the discerning qualities of the intellect. Impulse driven actions of the mind are weak and lead nowhere. Whereas decisions born out of the intellect are rooted in common sense and lead to your goal. These facts have to be kept in mind in practically all facets of life including the financial facet. If you trust your intellect you are a sure winner. But beware of your fickle mind which can make you lose even what is rightfully yours.

Believe It or Not

Strange to say my mother who had always been critical of me and my way of talking and doing things suddenly felt sad for me. She told me that what I had done was not really my fault. I was completely floored by her new attitude. Since she was totally attached to my children she promised me a plot of land on which I could build a small house. Unfortunately she could not keep her promise. However she gave me a sizeable amount of money which was solely meant to put food on the table in later years. She also promised to make arrangements for the children's higher education.

But unfortunately she told me that I myself should invest the money and not disturb other family members. So I invested the money with someone I had known for over thirty years without seeking anyone's advice. I did not even discuss this matter with close friends.

Believe it or not, this man with whom I had invested my money passed away recently. Now I am running from pillar to post trying to retrieve at least some amount from his family. Up to now, I have not succeeded.

No doubt my mother was generous, but asking me to make an investment without consulting other family members was the last nail on the coffin. How could she allow a person who had committed such disastrous financial mistakes to use her head to invest such precious money, money that is very much needed today? However once again I acted in an irresponsible way and once again my family has to pay the price.

CHILDREN

They are the silver linings in
our dark clouds
They are the roses between
the thorns
They are the oases in our
deserts
They are the brightest stars
in our private skies
They are our friends and
even philosophers -- if we let
them be.

Tread ever so softly, for
you tread on your
children's dreams

The Calm Before the Storm

*S*o much water has gone under the bridge. I don't want to play the blame game, nor do I want to sensationalise my marriage. Relationships that have failed remain with us like a ton of bricks for a long time. They upset our physical well being, cause problems in the family and play havoc with our emotions. Maybe there was a reason for this upheaval. Sometimes two people are very nice individually, but put them together and it's a catastrophe. Maybe that's what happened with both of us. We came from completely different backgrounds. I was attached to my parents but he was obsessed with his mother. He had lost his father while still at college. His mother supported him until the day he began to earn, so he felt he owed her a lot.

Besides our children we had another great bond – Shirdhi Sai Baba. He was the great peace maker between both of us. Thursday, Baba's day was so dear to us. We would be at Baba's temple without fail, every week. We often travelled to Shirdhi in the State of Maharashtra where Baba once lived and where he rests today in a magnificent mandir (temple). We took our kids, I think, five times to Shirdhi. We loved Baba so much and we thought he loved us too. But now, I wonder if Baba loved us enough.

It was really a tumultuous time when our children were growing up. But we did not give up hope. We tried to make things work out, especially for the sake of the children. My elder son had made it clear that he wanted both parents and was not willing to sacrifice one for the other.

I must give credit to my husband for going to great lengths to save our marriage. Ultimately he succeeded and we managed to get past all the things that had happened. Soon both our children were grown up simultaneously.

We became members of two of the most prestigious clubs in the city. Becoming members of the Madras Gymkhana was like coming back home.

We had a lovely home and were travelling quite a bit. Going to movies as a family was a lot of fun. Thank God, I thought, we are finally out of the woods. And then Fate stuck its deadliest blow.

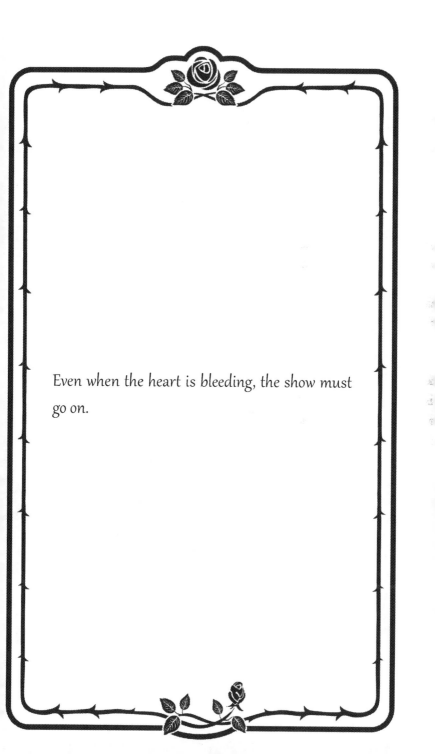

Even when the heart is bleeding, the show must go on.

When Love is not Enough

Sometimes the medical fraternity will not give you the facts about certain situations and sometimes they have every right to withhold such information. It is in the patient's interest that this is done. But what about psychiatric tablets? Should not the patient and family be told about the side effects of such tablets? Don't they have the right to this information?

My elder son who suffered from mild depression decided to go in for counselling. The concerned neuropsychiatrist was very well known in the city and handled many young people. He put my son on a heavy dose of medicine which his body could not tolerate. So the dose was lowered. My son had just returned from abroad where he was doing his Masters. The doctor's father, even better known, was an experienced neurologist, and was not keen on sending him back abroad as he was on anti depressants. But his son thought that such a decision would adversely affect my son's future and gave him permission to resume his Masters. He was given a prescription with the words "weekly review by email" at the bottom of the paper. Strangely enough, neither my son nor I noticed this postscript.

I had taken four opinions for the removal of a single wisdom tooth for my son. But I did not take even a second opinion about these anti-depressants. And I did not ask about side effects nor did the doctor educate me. Some three months down the line my son called me and told me that his medicine was getting over. I immediately called the doctor and told him about this message. He told me to ask my son to email him. This message was immediately communicated. Unfortunately that very day the Internet was cut in my son's residence by the landlord since one of the flat mates had very foolishly sublet the apartment. The following day I actually forgot about the email. Further, that the shortage of medicine could have been caused by an overdose did not cross my mind. And in all honesty the doctor did not caution me about such an eventuality. Instead I was worried about withdrawal systems. So I purchased the tablets and forwarded it to my son. But it was too late.

Suddenly out of the blue, we got a call from the Indian Embassy early one morning. We were told not to leave the house that day. We rang up some one very close to our family about the call. He knew immediately that it was bad news. About an hour later he walked in to our house. He was forced to give us the news. Our beloved elder son was no more. We were suddenly confronted with something we had subconsciously thought could happen only to others, but never to us. But it happened to our family! It took nearly ten days "to send him home". We got the autopsy report. It was so graphic, perfect to the last detail. I believe that is how it's done in the US. They bled him. They actually bled my son. They conducted the autopsy only after every single drop of that precious blood was drained from his body. Afterwards they embalmed him. We went through an agonizing ten days before he "arrived home" in a freezer box. My child, whom I had seen off at the airport hardly four months back, was brought home in a Freezer Box!

The wife of one of my cousins tranquilized me so strongly that I lost any semblance of feelings. I was totally numb. I did not cry at my own son's funeral. And someone actually commented to me that I seemed to have taken the tragedy pretty well. That was my son and I felt nothing. Something was gnawing inside my heart but I just did not know what to do. Something was terribly wrong but I was so calm. I just sat and kept looking at him. Then they lifted him out of that box and placed him outside the house on a palm mat. The hand that had fed him was forced to put raw rice into his silent mouth. After that he was placed in some van, I think. I kept looking at him in that vehicle and even then I did not understand the horrendous enormity of the tragedy. Then the men took him away to perform the final rites at a crematorium. My son at a crematorium! There he was reduced to ashes that were strewn into a hungry ocean. So much love, so much goodness, so much compassion – gone just like that!

Only then it struck me – that had been my beloved son lying in that ice box. I wanted to see him once more. I had to see him just once more. I just wanted a glimpse of that precious face! But it was not to be. He was gone forever. I could never see my son again. The agony was unbearable. I could not believe what had happened. People tried to comfort me, they meant well. Some people told me that I was not alone in my grief. So many people had lost precious children. Others even told me that I must get on with my life. One friend gave me six months and only six months to mourn. Six months for a beloved son. I could not comprehend his logic.

My husband really believes he is with the Lord. I believe nothing. All I know is that I will never see him again. I stopped going out except when absolutely necessary. It took me six years to attend a family get together. Behind every smile on my face he is there. When I fill my car at the gas station I see him in the adjoining Super Market, one of his favourite places. When I go to the club I remember him. When I go to bed he is there, when I get up he is there. His body, silent and lifeless in that Freezer Box haunts me to this day and will do so till the end of my time. Even people close to me, except my late mother, are not aware of my feelings. They think I have moved on. I have moved on – with the help of medication.

They say that the past must be forgotten. But not in such cases. I want to remember everything that concerned him. I want to remember all the times, both good and bad, that I spent with him. Why did this happen? I am searching for an answer but I know in my heart that I will never find one. And time does not heal. Time only covers the wound superfluously. But underneath, it festers and it hurts like hell. But no one will know. I believe I could have done better as a mother, especially during his childhood.

I did not spend enough time with him. When he wanted to play with me I was too "busy". But I loved him.

I did not try to be his confidante when he was very young. I was too obsessed with my "problems". But I loved him.

I did not bother to find out why he was working so late at nights. But I loved him.

I believed more in medication than in good nutrition. But I loved him.

As a child he wanted me to read to him... I did not. But I loved him.

He was my Breath.

He was my Heart Beat.

But I did not do enough.

And from the ashes to rise again

Through the dust, to breathe again

Epilogue

I have laid bare this life of mine and created this book especially for you, my readers. I hope you felt a personal connection with these stories, with the joys and sorrows, and learnt lessons from my experiences. When my elder son passed away my sorrow was so profound I wanted to stop living. In fact, a driver of ours who had once worked for our family came home and enquired whether I was still alive. He did not believe that I could survive this loss since he was aware of the deep love I had for my son.

My son was a masterpiece gifted by god to us. They say those whom the Gods love die young. I have no faith in these words. He had so much to live for and to have lost him at twenty three was a tragedy beyond words. But what could I do? How much could I cry? Even if we take an inventory of our life and assess the pros and cons, not all the blessings can outweigh the magnitude of the loss. Nevertheless we have to take the inventory, maybe a few years after the tragedy. We have to count the blessings, we have to be grateful. Only then can we do justice to our family members who depend upon us for strength. We have to thank God for our family and friends who stood with us in our darkest hours.

Today I am happy that I am alive mainly for the sake of my family. And especially for the sake of my younger son, who is my light at the end of the tunnel. He has brought me to a place I never imagined I could reach. He was just eighteen when tragedy struck our family. My husband and I were totally devastated, and so was he. But he could not immerse himself in sorrow. He literally carried us through the pain and heartache. In fact all the documents and even the autopsy report were directed to his email. He had to deal with all the graphic accounts of what had supposedly happened to his elder brother.

I thought that life will never have any meaning, any more. But now I realise that there is meaning in every small thing, only we have to find it. The pain will never go away, and it will hurt unbearably sometimes. But we have to grasp the smallest straw within our reach. In my case if medication is necessary, so be it.

I treasure the memories of the years I had him. As I have written earlier, the pain is always there and the wound heals only superfluously. But Time teaches you to live with the sorrow. You understand the value of life, of people, of the smallest family get together.

I often feel the negativity in the early years of my marriage may have been a cause for my son's depression. I was too obsessed with myself and wasted precious time on assumptions that were probably not grounded in reality. May be my moment of self realisation came too late. I must admit that my husband has stood by me in all the highs and lows of my life. I should have realised that life has both hits and misses. We can't all take home awards, but we can definitely put in our best performance at the show, the show in this case being life itself. Why on earth did I not appreciate all the positives in my life? Why did I perceive the glass as half empty when it was actually half full? The Lord had blessed us with the greatest of all gifts - two amazing children. Can I ever see my elder son again? Can I ever hold that sunburnt hand again? Can I ever ruffle that lovely hair again? Can I ever catch him smiling to himself ever again?

I really hope a lot of young people will read my book. I hope it impacts them in the right way. And for those who grieve, who are faced with the greatest of all heart breaks, the loss of a child, I hope they will find the courage to live again. Remember what I was also told, that we are not alone in our grief. A million hearts have broken in sorrow and yet life continues. Only when we descend to the very depths of pain can we understand the suffering of other human beings. We are sadder no doubt, but wiser. It is a known fact of life, a very sad fact of life, that only when tragedy strikes us do we look deeply into life. Don't turn away from the pain. Don't run away. Face the torture in all its horror. Be grounded and let the pain take over you. One day it will release you. You will never forget but you would have withstood your darkest hour. You will learn to live again. You have no choice.

Through the anguish, through the tears try to see the infinitely rich beauty of the world that still exists. At least for the rest of your lives try to find the beauty. No doubt it is a tarnished beauty, tarnished by sorrow. But Time will clean the tarnish, not completely, but enough to enable you to see and appreciate. Trivia will no longer matter to a heartbroken soul.

This is definitely not an attempt to glorify loss but rather a heart wrenching attempt to come to terms with the fleeting nature of existence.

Remember Shelley's immortal words

"I fall upon the thorns of life

I bleed------"

Some people will fall upon the thorns of life. They will bleed. But should everyone?

Now that I have gone
The birds sing no more
And the roses have all faded
You write to me
Remember the time
I asked for a smile
And you said
You would think about it
Remember the time
I asked for an hour
And you said
An hour would cost you
A handful of dollars
Remember the time
I asked you to build a dream for me
And you said
You were not made that way
The years rolled by
And I learnt to live
Without that smile
Without that hour
Without that dream
And even if the birds sing no more
And the roses have all faded
Now that I have gone
I HAVE GONE